Cetus

Chamaeleon

Corona Borealis

Leo

Volans

Libra

Pisces

Cygnus

To Mum, thank you for your steady guidance
and bright and loving presence.

— C.A.

To Ping Wang, a mindful woman with a heart as bright
as the stars, who just happens to be my mom.

— W.T.

This edition published in 2025 by Flying Eye Books Ltd.
27 Westgate Street, London, E8 3RL.
www.flyingeyebooks.com

Represented by: Authorised Rep Compliance Ltd. Ground Floor,
71 Lower Baggot Street, Dublin, D02 P593, Ireland.
www.arccompliance.com

Text © Catherine Ard 2025
Illustrations © Wenjia Tang 2025

Catherine Ard has asserted her right under the Copyright, Designs and Patents Act, 1988,
to be identified as the Author of this Work. Wenjia Tang has asserted her right under the
Copyright, Designs and Patents Act, 1988, to be identified as the Illustrator of this Work.

All rights reserved. No part of this publication may be reproduced or transmitted in any form
or by any means, electronic or mechanical, including photocopying, recording or by any
information and storage retrieval system, without prior written consent from the publisher.
No part of this book may be used or reproduced in any manner for the purpose of training
artificial intelligence technologies or systems. Flying Eye Books Ltd expressly reserves
Wish Upon a Star from the text and data mining exception, in accordance with Article 4
of European Parliament Directive (EU) 2019/790.

Edited by Christina Webb
Designed by Maisy Ruffels
Star expert Ben Maughan

1 3 5 7 9 10 8 6 4 2

UK ISBN: 978-1-83874-210-2

Printed in China on FSC® certified paper.

Catherine Ard • Wenjia Tang

WISH UPON A STAR

The Science, Magic and Meaning of Stars

Flying Eye Books

Contents

WHAT IS A STAR?

A Star Is Born 10

Types of Star 12

When a Star Dies 14

Exploding Stars 16

Galaxies 18

The Milky Way 20

LOOKING UP

Constellations 24

Ancient Stargazers 26

Astronomers 28

Deep-Space Discovery 30

STORIES IN THE SKY

Heroes in the Sky 34

Lighting the Way 36

Bridge of Star-Crossed Lovers 38

The Matariki Family 40

How Fisher Went to Skyland 42

Guardians of the Great Flood 44

STARS AND US

Celestial Navigation 48

Inspired by Stars 50

Symbols of Faith 52

Star Signs 54

Show Time 56

Starry Superstitions 58

Glossary & Index 60

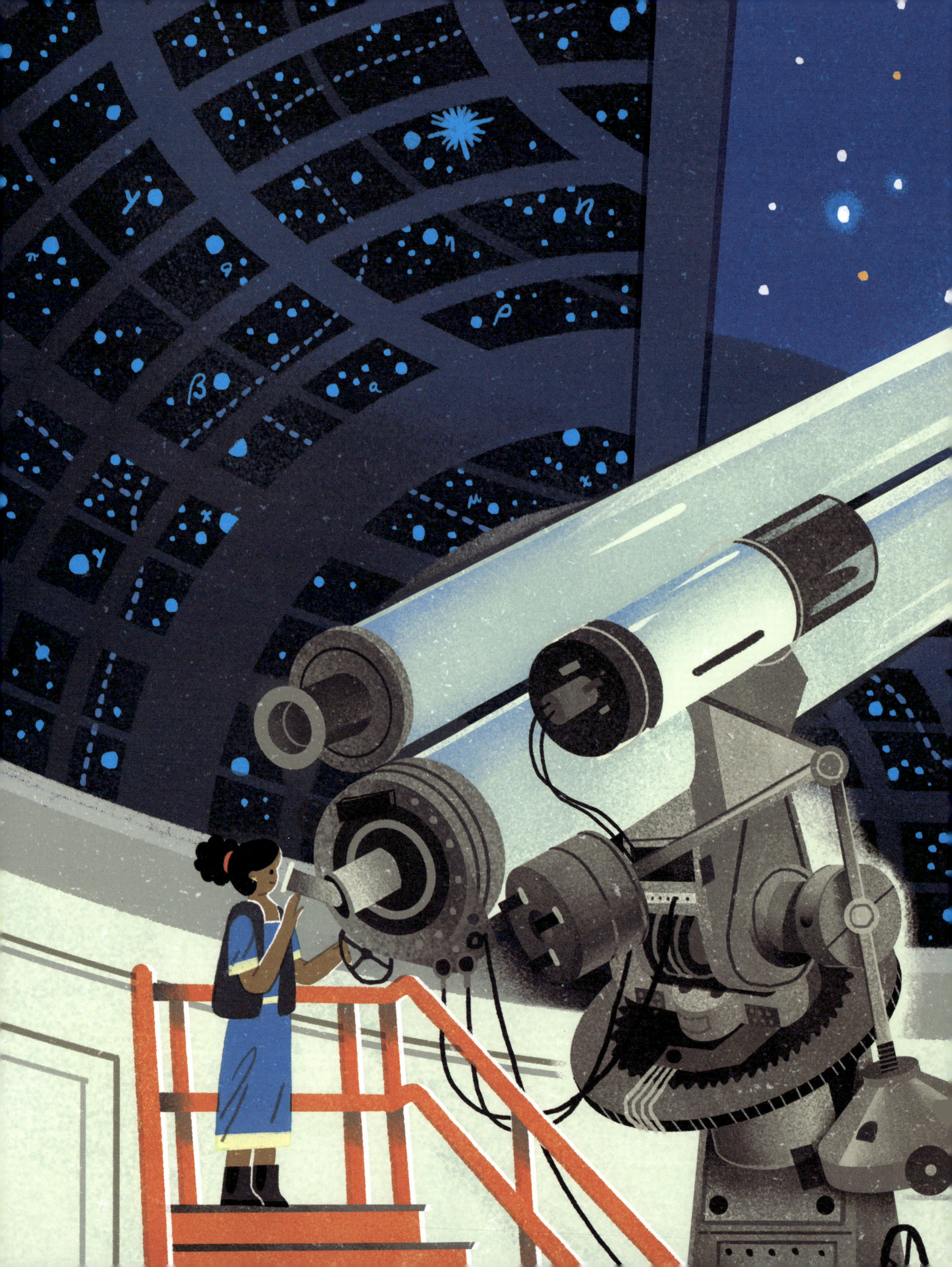

WHAT IS A STAR?

On a clear night you can see what lies far beyond our world. Each tiny spot of twinkling light in the inky black sky is a star. A huge fiery ball made of **gases**, burning brightly trillions of miles away.

A Star Is Born

Just like us, stars have a life cycle. They are born, grow old over millions or billions of years and eventually die. The lives of these giant burning balls begin as little specks of dust.

Dusty space

Big clouds of dust float around between stars and form inside them. The dust is then either shed and carried off or blasted out in giant explosions when an old star dies.

Eventually, the dust that comes from old stars combines with gases to form new ones. Stars, therefore, are made from recycled dust!

Star nurseries

Stars start out inside **nebulas** – swirling clouds of dust and the gases hydrogen and helium.

Slowly, dust and gas are drawn into a clump by gravity, the force that pulls all objects towards each other.

As the clump gets bigger, the gravity gets stronger.

Nuclear fusion is still occuring, while a new star, called a main sequence star, is born.

Millions of years later **nuclear fusion** 'starts', with about four billion billion billion billion tiny 'explosions' per second!

The clump gets so big it collapses. The centre fuses to form a **core** called a protostar.

Our star

There is one star that you can see from Earth during the day – the Sun! This bright ball of burning gases provides the light and heat that make life on Earth possible.

Solar flare
Bright flashes shoot hot gases out into space.

Solar tornado
Thousands of towering tornadoes form on the surface, each one big enough to swallow the Earth.

Bubbling hot
Giant bubbles rise up to the surface – each 1,000 km wide.

Distance: 93 million miles (150 km) from Earth
Age: four and half billion years old
Core temperature: 15 million °C
Surface temperature: 5,500°C
Size: 864,400 miles (1.4 million km) across

Types of Star

From Earth, all stars look alike: small, white and bright. Zoom in with a **telescope** and you can see that stars come in a variety of sizes and colours. Some shine brilliantly, while others gently glow.

Mass matters

Stars are measured by their mass. This is the total amount of matter, or stuff, in an object.

All grown up

For most of a star's lifetime they are settled in a stable stage as a main sequence star. Ninety per cent of the stars in the universe are main sequence stars, including the Sun. These stars vary in size, mass and brightness, but they are all doing the same thing: burning their fuel and releasing energy.

Fuel to burn

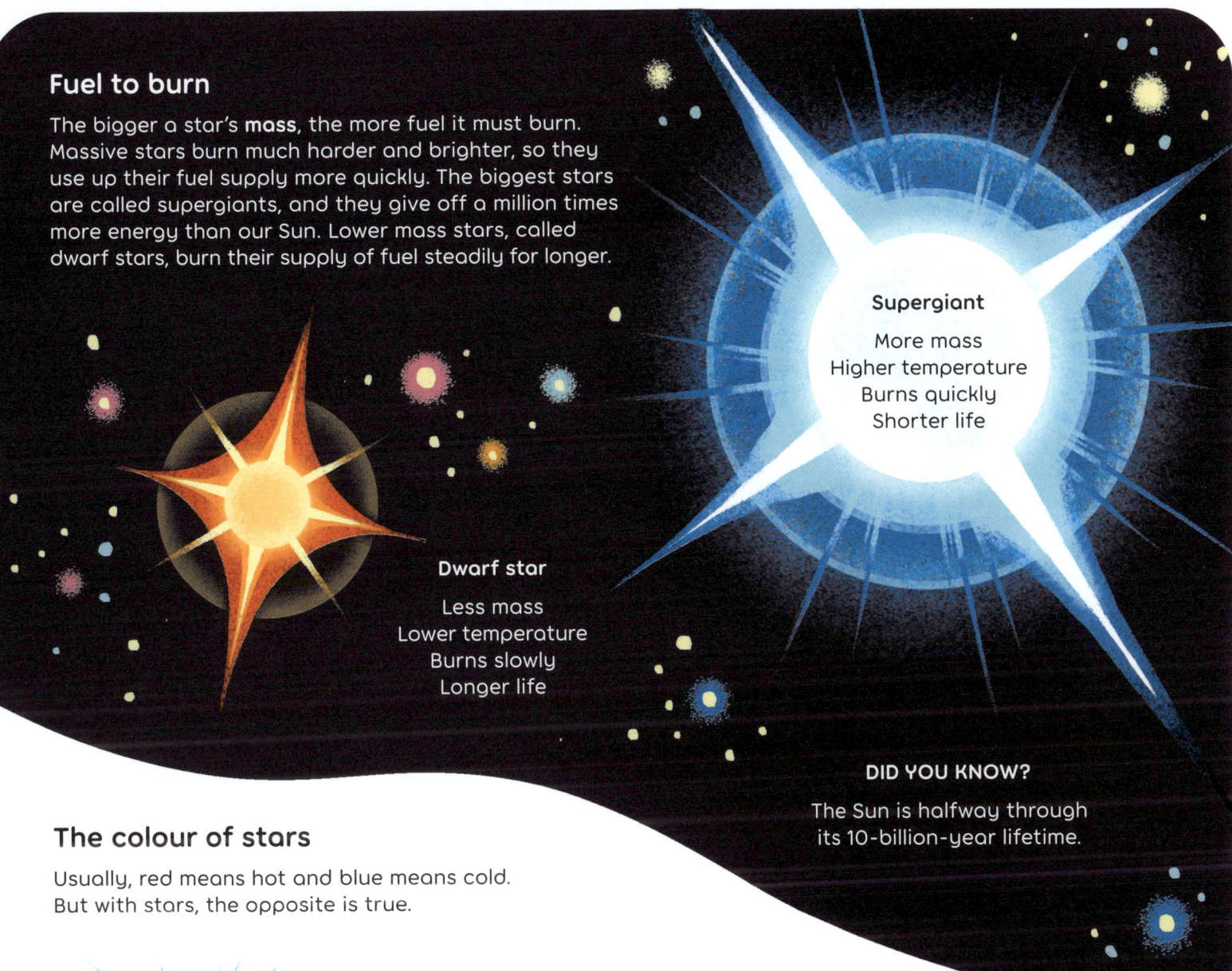

The bigger a star's **mass**, the more fuel it must burn. Massive stars burn much harder and brighter, so they use up their fuel supply more quickly. The biggest stars are called supergiants, and they give off a million times more energy than our Sun. Lower mass stars, called dwarf stars, burn their supply of fuel steadily for longer.

Supergiant
More mass
Higher temperature
Burns quickly
Shorter life

Dwarf star
Less mass
Lower temperature
Burns slowly
Longer life

DID YOU KNOW?
The Sun is halfway through its 10-billion-year lifetime.

The colour of stars

Usually, red means hot and blue means cold. But with stars, the opposite is true.

Blue or white stars are massive, hot and bright. They live for about 10 million years.

Yellow stars have medium mass, heat and brightness. They live for 50 million to 20 billion years.

Orange and red stars are usually smaller, cooler and dimmer. They can live for trillions of years.

Brown dwarf stars have such low mass they give off no visible light. Brown dwarfs never die.

High mass — Low mass

When a Star Dies

Stars meet different fates when they reach the end of their lives. Some quietly fade away, while others go out with a bang.

Main sequence stars

As a star runs out of fuel to burn, it swells and becomes a red giant. Red giants are bright, but cool. Gas and dust from the red giant escape into space, and the core of the red giant collapses to form a white dwarf.

Nebula

Main sequence star

Planetary nebula

Red giant

When a supermassive star dies, it forms a **black hole**.

Black hole

Supernova

White dwarf

White dwarfs are about the size of a planet, but they are hot and very dense. They faintly glow for billions of years. Eventually, a white dwarf cools down and stops shining. It becomes a black dwarf and is almost invisible.

Neutron star

Gas and dust are blasted out from a supernova to form wispy shapes that glow brightly for thousands of years. The remaining core shrinks to form a **neutron star**.

Wolf-Rayet star

These rare and spooky-looking stars occur when a massive star has a final burst of activity before it begins to die.

Massive stars

When a massive star runs out of fuel, it swells into a red supergiant. Its core contracts from the inside and then collapses, and the star explodes in a spectacular **supernova**.

Massive star

Red supergiant

Hybrid star

Astronomers believe that occasionally there could be a star hiding inside a star! When a red supergiant swells up it may swallow a nearby neutron star, making the supergiant shine even brighter.

Exploding Stars

After millions of years of shining brightly, massive stars blow apart in the biggest explosions in the universe. They then shrink into the darkest, densest things in the universe.

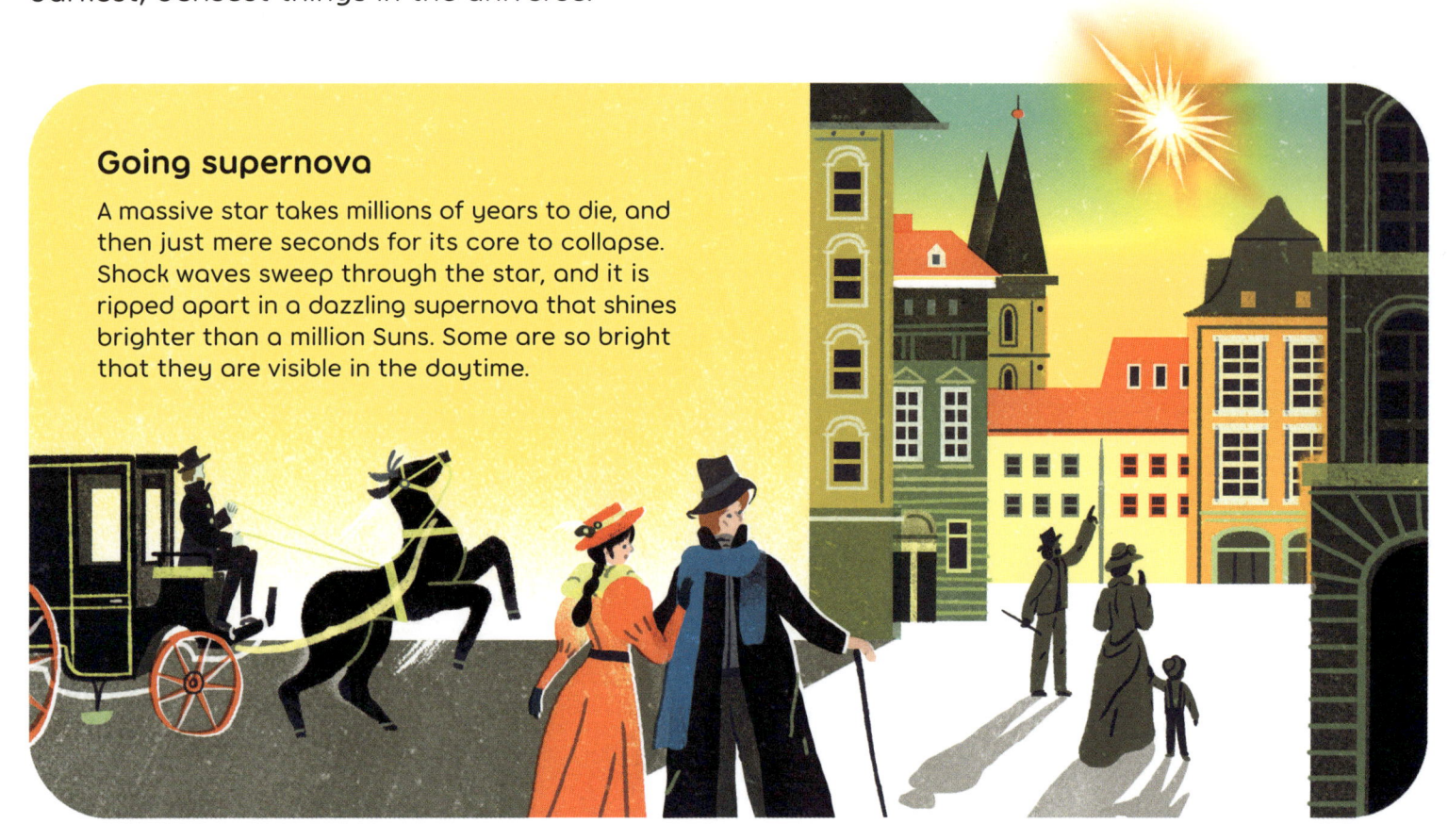

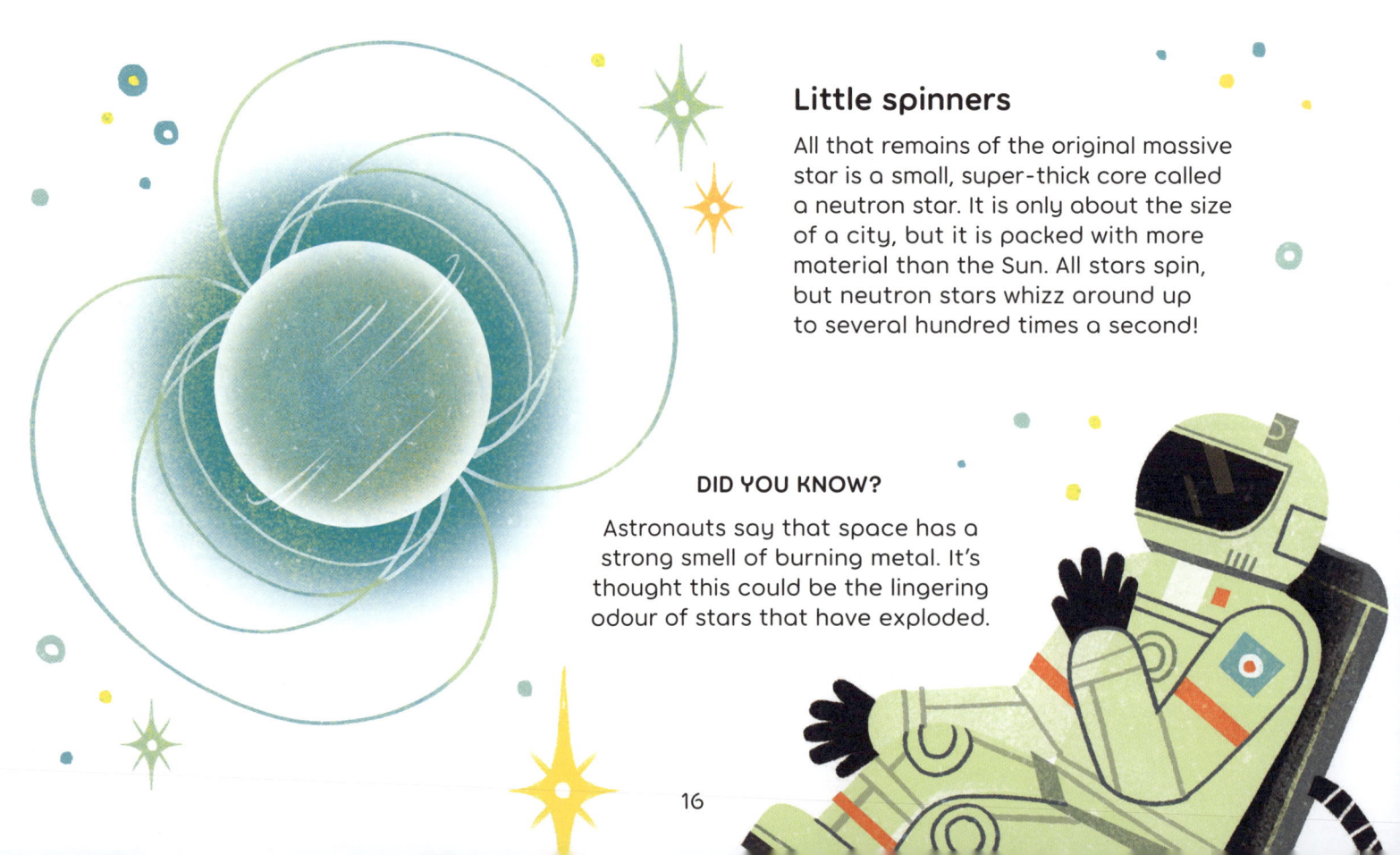

Going supernova

A massive star takes millions of years to die, and then just mere seconds for its core to collapse. Shock waves sweep through the star, and it is ripped apart in a dazzling supernova that shines brighter than a million Suns. Some are so bright that they are visible in the daytime.

Little spinners

All that remains of the original massive star is a small, super-thick core called a neutron star. It is only about the size of a city, but it is packed with more material than the Sun. All stars spin, but neutron stars whizz around up to several hundred times a second!

DID YOU KNOW?

Astronauts say that space has a strong smell of burning metal. It's thought this could be the lingering odour of stars that have exploded.

Beaming blinkers

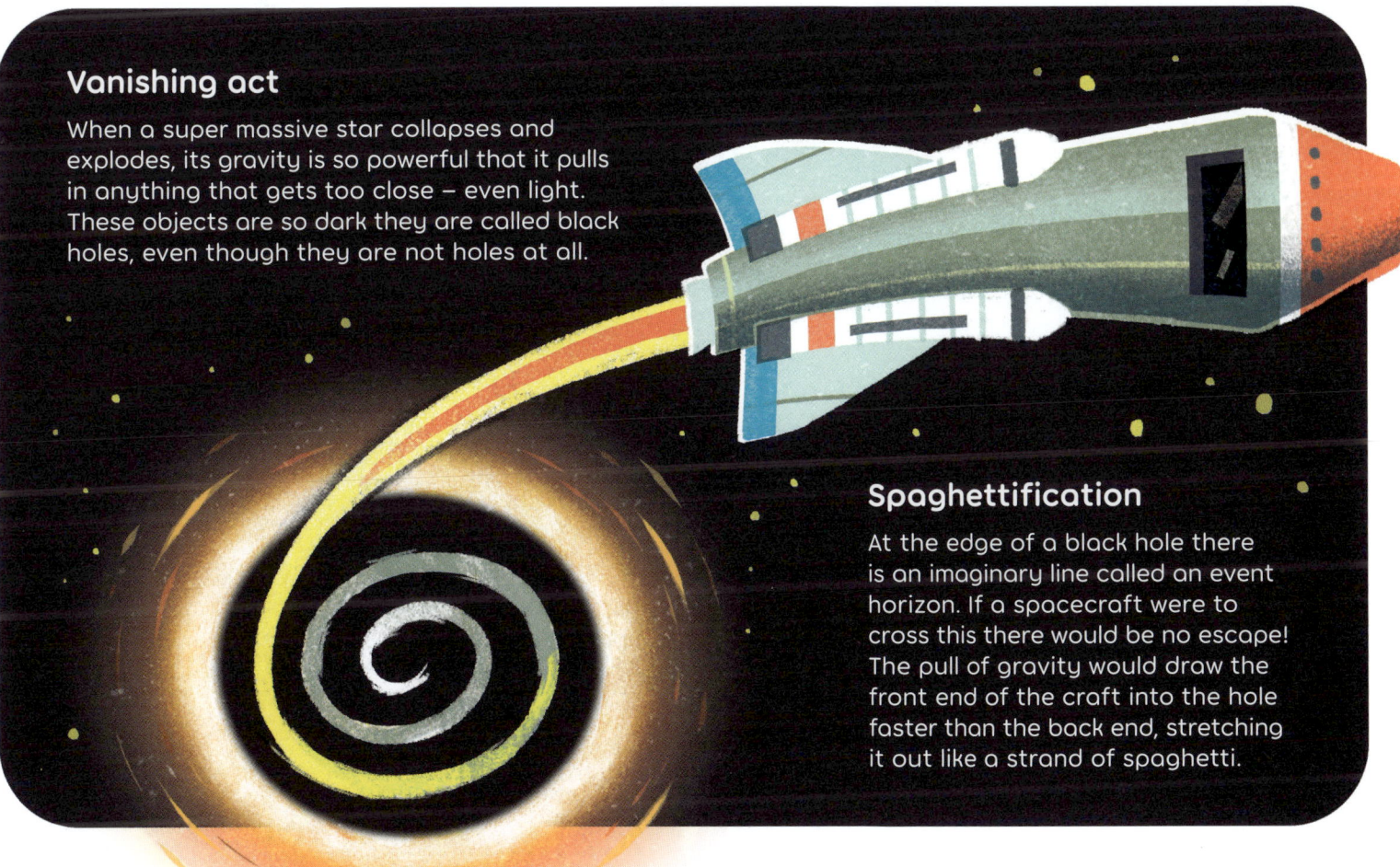

Some neutron stars become **pulsars**. These stars have a stream of energy blasting out in two opposite beams. As the star spins, its beams sweep around, like a lighthouse. From Earth it looks as though its light is blinking on and off. When they were first discovered it was considered that they could be signals from aliens!

Vanishing act

When a super massive star collapses and explodes, its gravity is so powerful that it pulls in anything that gets too close – even light. These objects are so dark they are called black holes, even though they are not holes at all.

Spaghettification

At the edge of a black hole there is an imaginary line called an event horizon. If a spacecraft were to cross this there would be no escape! The pull of gravity would draw the front end of the craft into the hole faster than the back end, stretching it out like a strand of spaghetti.

Galaxies

The universe is unimaginably big. The smudges of light in the sky are not stars, but galaxies, each one containing between a million and a trillion stars. There are at least 100 billion galaxies – that's a lot of stars!

What is a galaxy?

A **galaxy** is a huge, spinning collection of gas, dust and stars held together by the pulling force of gravity. Galaxies come in different shapes and sizes.

Spiral

Over 60 per cent of the galaxies that have been discovered are spiral. They have flat discs with a bulge in the middle and spiral arms like a giant pinwheel, and shine brightly with lots of new stars.

Elliptical

The largest known galaxies are elliptical (oval-shaped) and contain up to a trillion stars.

Stretched oval

These galaxies shine less brightly and have lots of older stars.

Irregular

These galaxies are often the smallest, with no recognisable shape. They shine brightly and are made up of many young stars.

Lenticular

This is a flat galaxy with a central bump-like disc and no spiral arms.

Galaxy glue

Scientists believe that an invisible substance, called **dark matter**, holds galaxies together. This ghostly stuff is thought to spread all through galaxies and even out beyond their stars like an invisible mist, providing the gravity needed to keep stars from flying off into space.

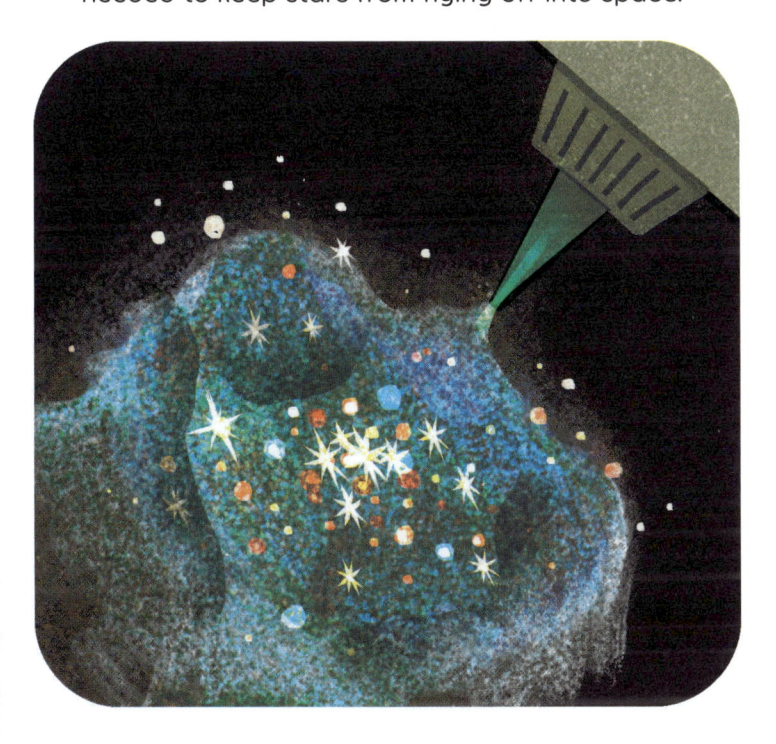

Supersized

Galaxies are huge, but they are not the biggest things in space. Galaxies are grouped in **clusters**, which are grouped within superclusters! In between the clusters are big empty areas of nothing.

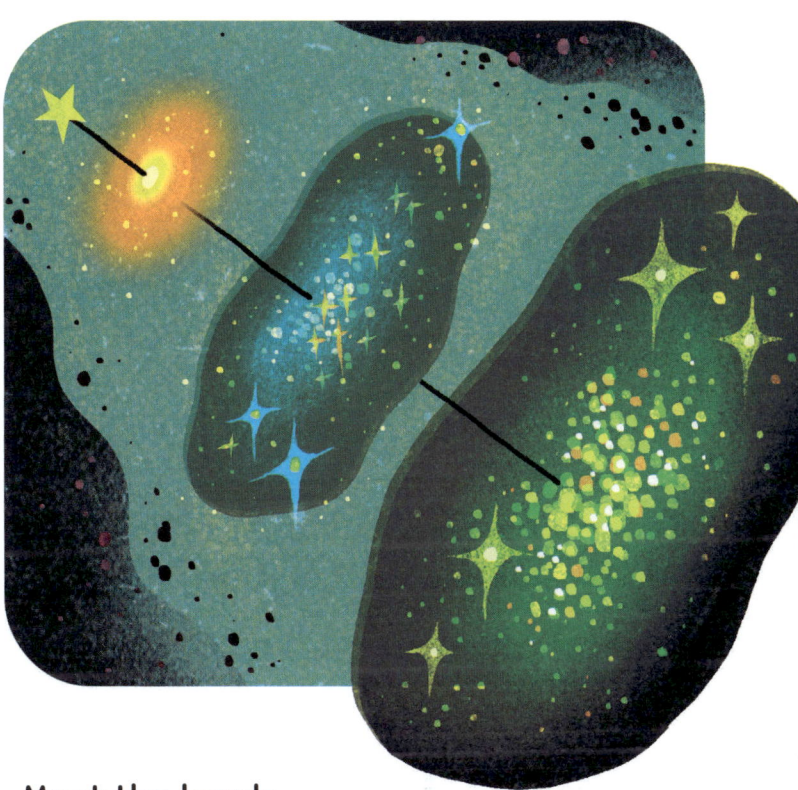

Collision course

Galaxy collisions occur when moving galaxies collide into one another. They happen in slow-motion over millions of years. Stars are so spread out within a galaxy that two galaxies can merge without causing any **cosmic** crashes.

Meet the locals

Earth sits inside the Milky Way galaxy, which is part of a cluster of 54 galaxies known as the Local Group.

DID YOU KNOW?

In about four billion years, the Milky Way is expected to collide with our neighbouring galaxy Andromeda.

The Milky Way

Welcome to our little corner of space. The Milky Way is a medium-sized spiral galaxy made up of more than 100 billion stars. Earth, the Sun and the planets of our **Solar System** are a tiny speck nestled inside one of the Milky Way's giant arms.

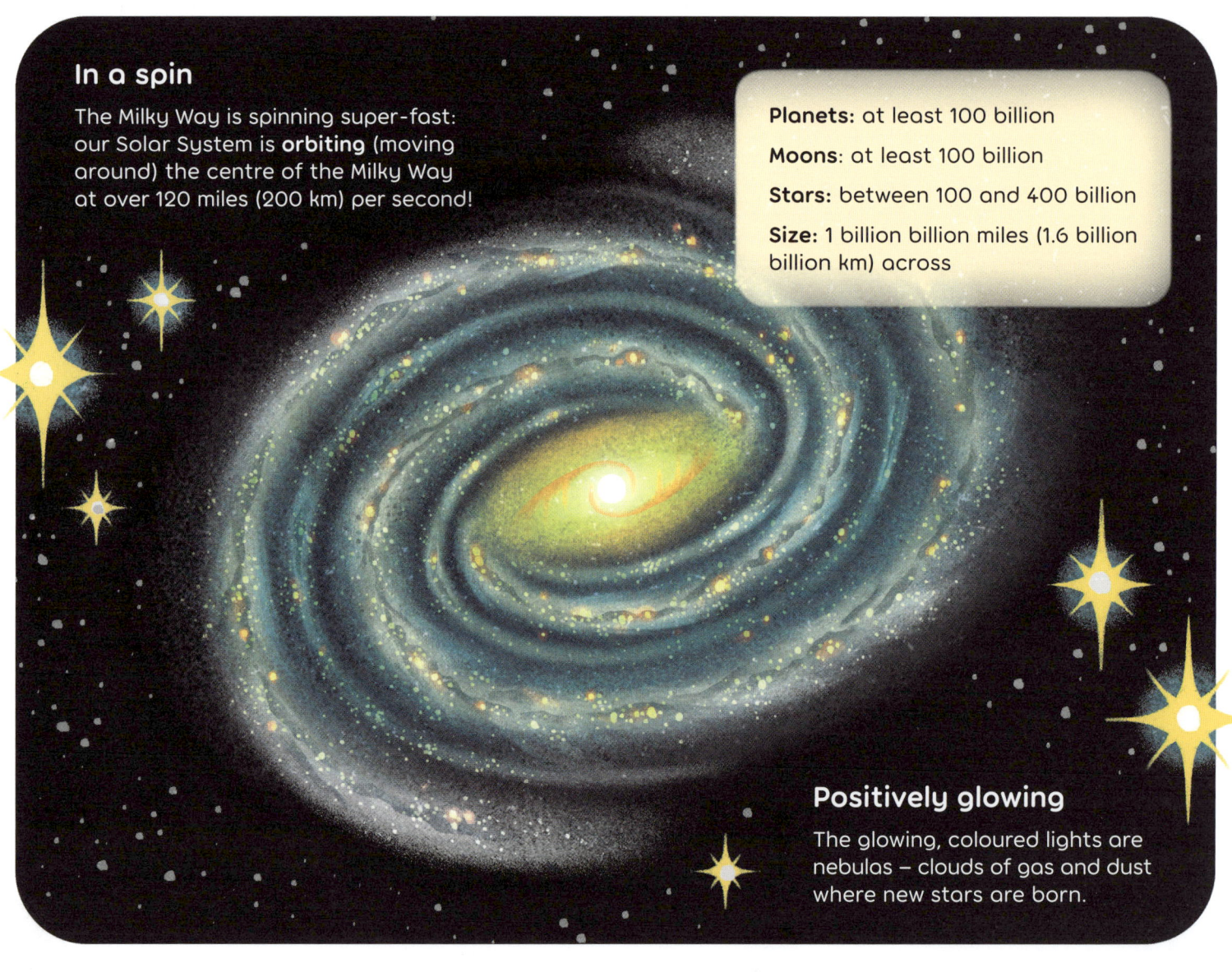

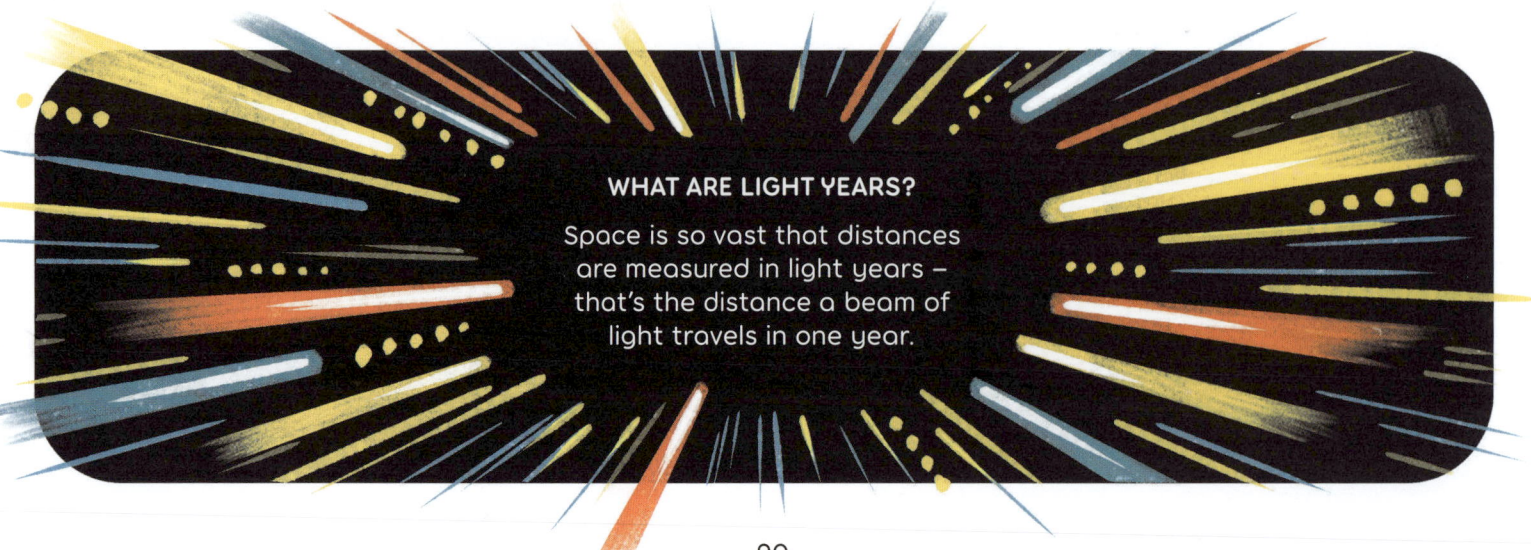

In a spin
The Milky Way is spinning super-fast: our Solar System is **orbiting** (moving around) the centre of the Milky Way at over 120 miles (200 km) per second!

Planets: at least 100 billion

Moons: at least 100 billion

Stars: between 100 and 400 billion

Size: 1 billion billion miles (1.6 billion billion km) across

Positively glowing
The glowing, coloured lights are nebulas – clouds of gas and dust where new stars are born.

WHAT ARE LIGHT YEARS?
Space is so vast that distances are measured in light years – that's the distance a beam of light travels in one year.

Spilled milk

The Milky Way gets its name from the way it looks to us on Earth. On a clear night, stars of the other arms of the galaxy appear as a band of speckled light that looks like milk splashed across the sky!

DID YOU KNOW?

The Milky Way is known by different names around the world. In China it is called 'Silver River'. The people of the Kalahari Desert that runs through Botswana, Namibia and South Africa call it 'Backbone of the night'.

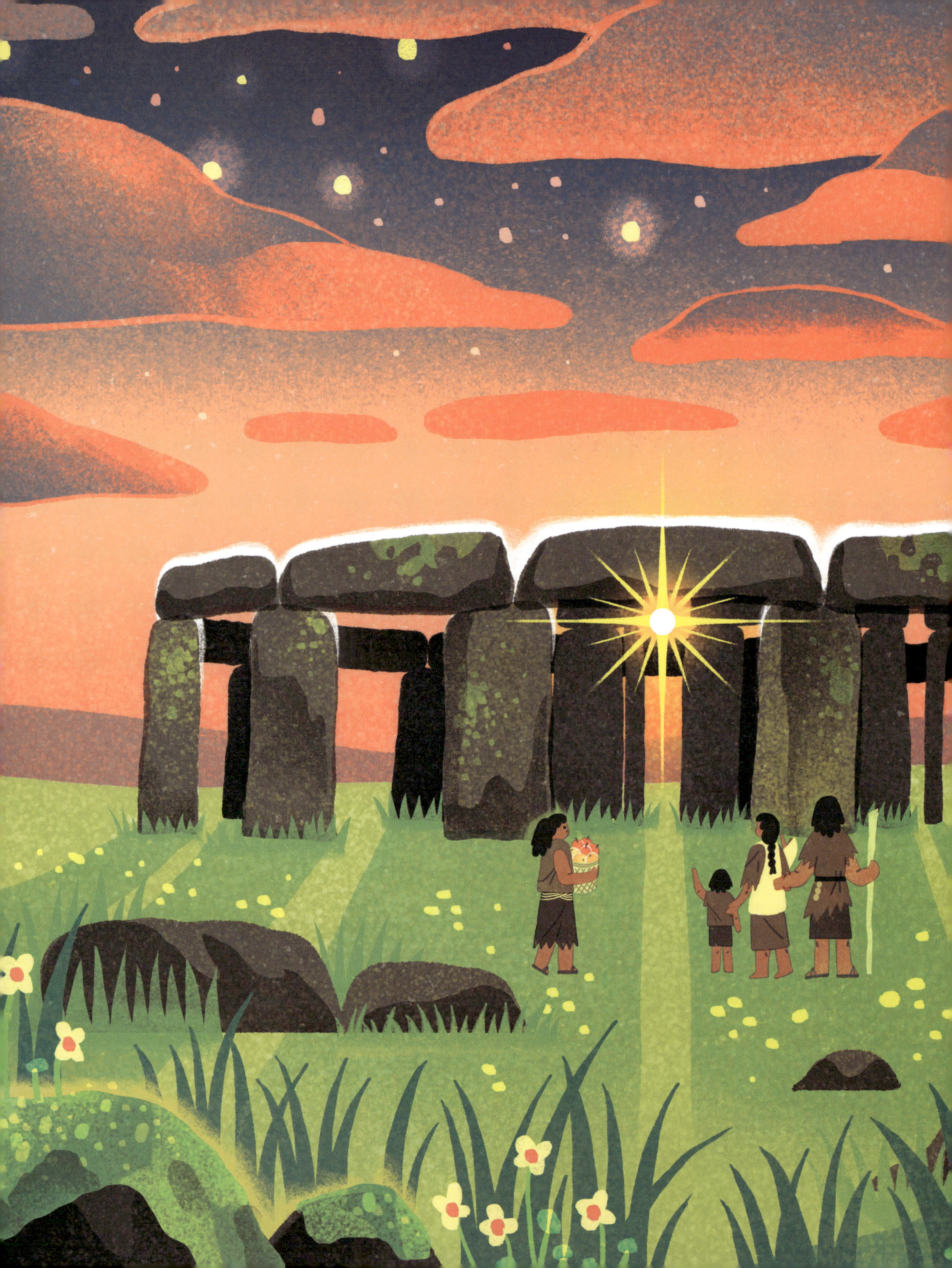

LOOKING UP

Ever since people have lived on Earth, they have gazed up at the sky and wondered about their place in the universe. Humans know more now than ever before, but we are still filled with awe when looking up.

Constellations

The stargazers of ancient times crafted stories to explain the glittering objects that moved across the sky each night.

Join the dots

Groups of the brightest stars in the sky can be joined up with invisible lines to form animals, people and objects. We call these shapes **constellations**. They are easy to recognise and have helped many people find their way in the dark.

Ancient constellations

Forty-eight of the constellations were picked out thousands of years ago by the people of Ancient Babylon (modern-day Iraq), Egypt and Greece. They were named after mythical characters, such as Orion, the hunter of Greek legend. There are also 12 constellations known as the **zodiac**. The Sun appears to pass in front of these 12 constellations over the course of the year.

Modern constellations

There are now 88 recognised constellations, and today they divide the sky into sections rather than shapes and characters. The sections all fit together like a jigsaw to make a sphere.

DID YOU KNOW?

Stars are shown in different sizes on a star chart to indicate their brightness.

North and South

Earth is divided into two **hemispheres**. Some constellations can be seen from both, but facing opposite ways. Others are completely different. This is because Earth's North Pole faces out into the universe, whereas the South Pole points close to the centre of the Milky Way galaxy.

Starry seasons

The constellations visible at night also depend on the season. Earth orbits the Sun once each year. Our view into space changes because Earth is in a different spot in its orbit each night.

Ancient Stargazers

Throughout history, **civilisations** developed different ways of making sense of the night sky. People looked to the stars and planets for guidance and saw cosmic events as warnings.

Cosmic timekeepers

Before calendars or clocks existed, people studied the Sun, Moon and stars to keep track of time. They knew when to sow and harvest crops by their positions in the sky.

Celestial cycles

Three hundred thousand years ago early humans tracked the phases of the Moon by carving on animal bones.

Sunlight and shadows

During the summer solstice, the longest day of the year, the Sun illuminates the north and east sides of the ancient pyramid of Chichén Itzá in Mexico. The other sides are left in shadow, splitting the monument in two.

The first timepiece

Three thousand years ago Ancient Egyptians invented sundials to tell the time. Using a vertical stick called a *gnomon*, they tracked the Sun's shadow to pinpoint different times of day with precision.

Lamps and nails

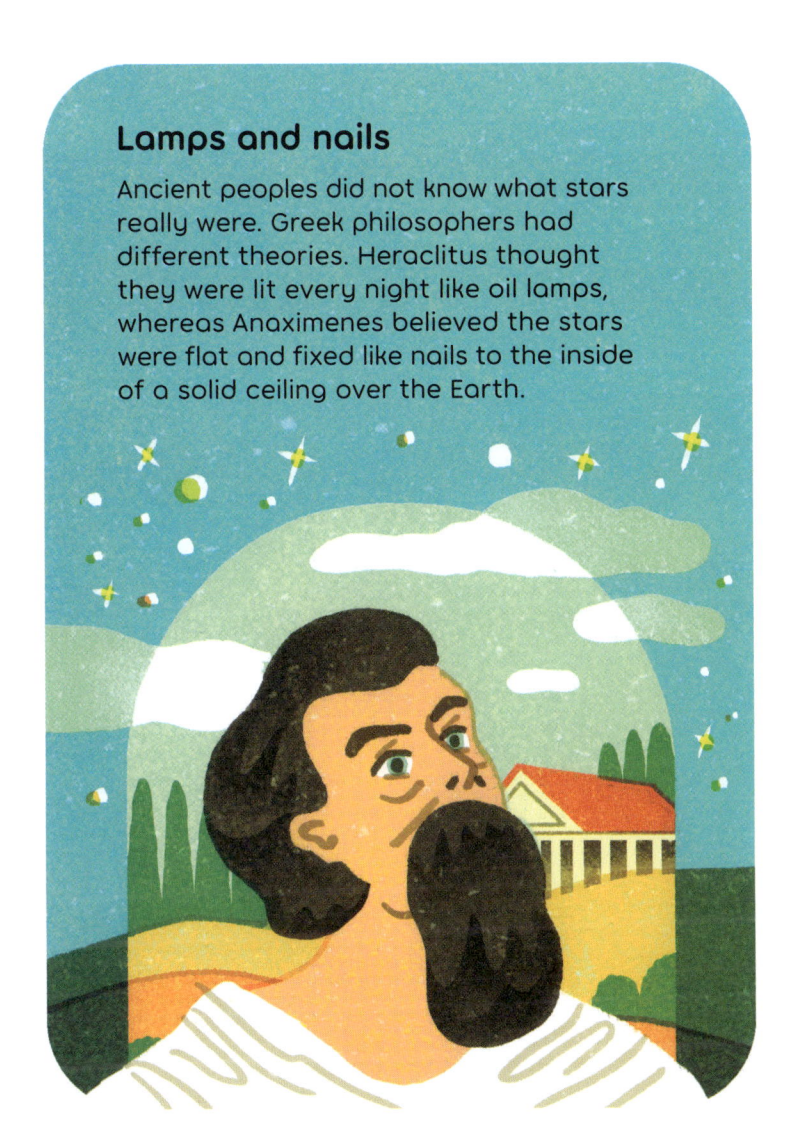

Ancient peoples did not know what stars really were. Greek philosophers had different theories. Heraclitus thought they were lit every night like oil lamps, whereas Anaximenes believed the stars were flat and fixed like nails to the inside of a solid ceiling over the Earth.

Signs from above

Without a scientific explanation to rely on, the disappearance of the Sun during a **solar** eclipse was seen by many ancient **civilisations** as a bad omen.

In Ancient China, eclipses were thought to be caused by a sky dragon eating the Sun. People would make loud noises to frighten the dragon away. In Ancient Inca culture, eclipses were a sign that the Sun god, Inti, was angry, and **sacrifices** were made to calm him.

Space forecast

Ancient civilisations used **astronomy** to predict cosmic events so that they could be prepared. An unexpected eclipse in the middle of a battle could lead to defeat.

Babylonian civilisation
4000 BCE (6,000 years ago)

Ziggurats were used as observatories. These tall pyramid-like buildings had a temple at the top to be near to the gods – and the stars.

Ancient China
1300 BCE (3,000 years ago)

Astronomers recorded 900 solar and 600 lunar eclipses over a period of 2,600 years.

Arabian civilisation
600 CE (1,500 years ago)

Many observatories were built where astronomers used huge instruments and mathematics to study the stars.

Astronomers

Over the past 500 years, our knowledge of stars has changed, and so have the ways in which we explore them. Each new generation of astronomers has built on the work of those who went before them.

Abu Ma'shar al-Balkhi (787–886 AD) created an early model showing planets moving around the Sun instead of the Earth.

Charles Messier (1730–1817) made a catalogue of stars and galaxies. Today, many objects are known by their Messier catalogue number – the Andromeda galaxy is M31.

Henrietta Swann Leavitt (1868–1921) discovered that the brightness of some stars is related to how often they pulse. This led astronomers to calculate the distances of stars and galaxies and the size of the Milky Way.

Sir Isaac Newton (1643–1727) discovered how gravity works and offered a theory about how objects move in space.

Benjamin Banneker (1731–1806) made important observations including an accurately predicted solar eclipse.

Annie Jump Cannon (1863–1941) classified around 350,000 stars.

Albert Einstein (1879–1955) published his 'theory of relativity' in 1915, explaining how gravity is related to the shape of the universe, and how black holes work.

Dorrit Hoffleit (1907–2007) devoted years to counting the stars visible with the naked eye – up to 9,096!

Edwin Hubble (1899–1953) proved that the universe was more than one galaxy, and that the Universe is still growing.

Jocelyn Bell Burnell (1943–) discovered the first pulsar – the rapidly spinning core of a dead star that sends pulses of radio waves out into space – in 1967.

Seeing into space: astronomy inventions

In 1609, Galileo Galilei built the first telescope for studying space, which led to observatories being built around the world.

In 1688, Sir Isaac Newton invented the first working, reflecting telescope by using a mirror instead of a lens.

In the 1840s, astronomers began to photograph the images picked up by their telescopes instead of sketching what they saw.

In 1937, Grote Reber built the first radio telescope, which could detect waves from distant space objects not visible to the human eye.

In 1962, the first space telescope, Ariel 1, was sent into orbit to take closer images of stars and planets.

Deep-Space Discovery

Hi-tech telescopes in space allow astronomers to see deeper into the cosmos than ever before. The images they send back are helping to solve mysteries about how the universe began.

Hubble Space Telescope

Launched in 1990, this space **observatory** orbits Earth every 95 minutes.

Ultraviolet (UV) Visible Light Infrared

Waves and rays

As well as the light that we can see, stars release other invisible waves and rays, such as the **UV** rays from the Sun that can cause sunburn. Between them, Hubble and Webb **satellites** can each spot a range of rays. For example, Webb's infrared vision can detect galaxies too distant or dusty for the Hubble telescope to see.

James Webb Space Telescope

Launched in 2021, this telescope orbits the Sun, 932,000 miles (1.5 million km) away from the Earth. Commands and information travel at the speed of light (186,000 miles per second/ 300,000 km per second), and take about five seconds to travel between the Webb telescope and Earth.

Travelling light

All the stars you see with your eyes are trillions of miles from Earth, and their light has taken billions of years to reach us. So, you are actually seeing stars from the past! The farther away an object is, the farther back in time you are looking.

DID YOU KNOW?

The **Big Bang** is the moment that our universe came into existence 13.8 billion years ago. It was already expanding at an incredible speed, as if it had come from a giant explosion. No one knows how the Big Bang started or if anything came before it. The Webb telescope is so powerful it can peer back and see the first stars and galaxies that formed after the Big Bang.

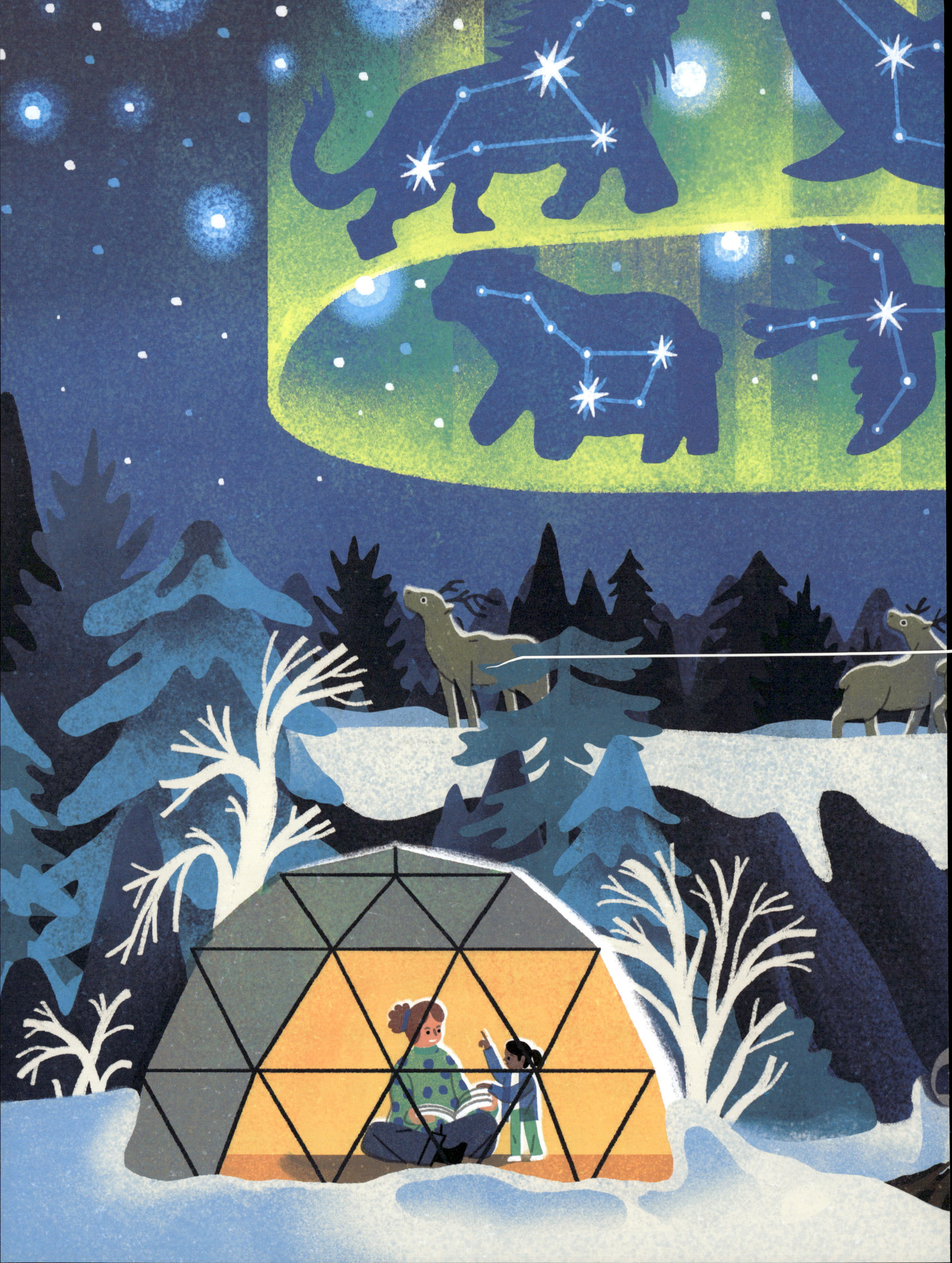

STORIES IN THE SKY

Floating above our heads while we sleep are tales about gods and heroes, spirits and wild beasts. Star stories are different around the world, but many share the same themes.

Heroes in the Sky

In Greek and Roman mythology, star constellations were heroes and beasts who were favoured by the gods. They were placed in the sky to shine for evermore as a reward for their greatness.

Andromeda's beauty

Andromeda was the only child of a king and queen who regularly boasted about her. One day, her mother declared, "Andromeda is even more lovely than the sea nymphs." When Poseidon, the sea god, heard this he was furious. He sent a flood and a giant sea serpent to destroy the kingdom.

Rescued from the rock

A priestess told the king to sacrifice his most precious possession to calm the sea god. So, the king and queen chained their beloved Andromeda to the cliff and left her to be devoured by the sea serpent. A brave prince called Perseus flew by on his winged sandals. At that moment, the sea serpent rose from the waves and Perseus plunged his sword into its heart. The monster fell down dead, and Andromeda was safely unshackled.

A place in the sky

Athena, the goddess of wisdom, promised to honour Andromeda with a place in the sky after her death. To see her, you must search for the shape of a chained maiden with outstretched arms in the night sky.

Scales of justice

In Roman mythology, Astraea is the goddess of justice and purity. Her name means 'star maiden' or 'starry sky'. Spurred on by humanity's increasing wickedness, Astraea was the last of the gods to leave Earth, becoming the Virgo constellation.

Lighting the Way

The different tribes of Southern Africa tell mythical tales about the brightest stars in the region. The stories reflect the lives of ancestors who hunted and grew food on the plains.

The hungry hunter

According to the Khoi people, a group of stars called the Khunuseti, or the Stars of Spring, were the daughters of the powerful sky god. One day, the stars told their husband to go out and hunt zebras. The husband set out, but he only took one arrow with him. He aimed and shot at the zebras, but missed and his arrow fell beyond them. He dared not return home without any meat, and he dared not retrieve his arrow because of a fierce lion that sat watching the zebras. To this day, he is stuck there in star form – hungry, thirsty and shivering with cold, unable to return, or to collect his arrow.

The road home

The IXam-ka tribe tells a story of a young girl in ancient times who wanted to light the way for people returning home from the fields at night. She scooped up a handful of ashes from the fire and flung it into the sky to make a glowing path. She then threw a meal of roasted roots into the sky, where the pieces now glow as red and white stars. Some people call her path the Milky Way, others know it as the Stars' Road.

The Sun in the sky

The IXam-ka also have a tale that explains how the Sun got into the sky. The Sun was originally a man whose underarms shone with beams of light. Unfortunately, he was lazy and would sleep late, selfishly keeping his light to himself and leaving the people cold. Children were sent to throw the sleeping Sun into the sky. Since then, his light and heat shines brightly for everyone in the world to enjoy.

Other tribes believed that every night the Sun was swallowed by a crocodile, and every morning it would appear from the crocodile's mouth.

Bridge of Star-Crossed Lovers

Ancient China had its own way of looking at the night sky. Many of the myths and legends that were told are still celebrated today, including this one.

The cowherd and the weaving maid

A young weaver girl worked for the sky goddess, the **Celestial Queen Mother**. One day, she and her six sisters came down to Earth, to bathe in a lake. A young cowherd saw them and picked up the clothes that one of them had left on the bank. When the sisters spotted him, six of them dressed quickly, turned into doves and flew back to the Celestial Palace. The weaver girl stayed behind to beg the cowherd to return her clothes. By the end of their conversation the pair had fallen completely in love. The weaver girl remained in the world and married the cowherd.

Forbidden love

The sky goddess was furious when she discovered that her servant had married a mortal, so she sent her troops to bring her back. As punishment, the weaver girl was made to weave the clouds in the sky for all eternity. The cowherd tried to reach his love, but the goddess took out her hairpin and scratched a wide river in the sky to separate the lovers forever.

A bridge of birds

The weaver girl and the cowherd are the stars Vega and Altair that sit on opposite sides of the river of stars – the Milky Way. Once a year, on the seventh night of the seventh Moon, all the magpies in the world take pity on the lovers and fly up into heaven to form a bridge over the river so that they can be together for one night.

DID YOU KNOW?

Every summer, this story is celebrated in the Qixi Festival – Chinese Valentine's Day. Lovers give each other gifts and look for the two stars in the sky.

The Matariki Family

Once a year, in midwinter, the star cluster known in Māori culture (indigenous New Zealand) as Matariki rises before dawn. It marks the beginning of a new year and a fresh start.

The eyes of god

According to Māori myth, Rangi, the sky father and Papa, the earth mother, were separated by their children, who longed for space between the earth and the sky. They forced their father into the heavens, and their mother towards the ground. One son, Tāwhirimātea, god of the winds, was so angry with his siblings for what they had done that he tore out his own eyes, crushed them in his hands and threw the pieces into the sky. The scattered pieces became stars. This constellation of stars is called Matariki, which means 'eyes of god'.

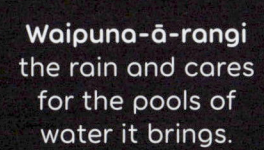

Waipuna-ā-rangi the rain and cares for the pools of water it brings.

Guiding stars

The Matariki stars also include a mother and her daughters. Each year they visit Mother Earth to help her prepare for the coming year. It is said that if the Matariki stars are dim, the next harvest will be poor. If the stars are bright, the harvest will be plentiful.

Hiwa-i-te-rangi brings the promise of the new season. The Māori would send her their wishes for the coming year.

Matariki, the mother, is the bringer of good fortune and health.

Waitā cares for the food that comes from the sea.

Waitī looks after living things that dwell in rivers, lakes and streams.

Pōhutukawa is connected to those who have passed away during the year.

Tupu-ā-nuku tends to plants that grow in the ground that can be picked or harvested for food.

How Fisher Went to Skyland

People have always wondered why the stars circle and return to the same position in the sky each year. The indigenous Anishinaabek community of Canada and America saw this as an animal who took annual travels around the North Star.

Sun seekers

Long, long ago, it was always winter. The animals knew that summer existed somewhere, but it never came to them. One year, Squirrel said to Fisher, 'Go to the place where the sky meets the Earth. There, the sky people are keeping summer to themselves. Go and bring warmth back.' Fisher agreed and set out for Skyland with his bravest friends – Otter, Lynx and Wolverine. The four travelled through the snow to the mountains. They climbed higher and higher until they reached the peak that touched the clouds.

Discovering Skyland

Otter and Lynx tried and failed to break through the sky. Then it was Wolverine's turn. He struck the sky again and again until he had made a crack. With one final leap he broke through into Skyland. Fisher jumped through after him.

Skyland was a beautiful place. It was warm and sunny, and plants and flowers grew everywhere. The warmth began to seep through to the land below, melting the snow.

Summer

When the sky people realised what was happening, they attacked with arrows. Wolverine escaped back through the hole, but Fisher knew that if he didn't make the hole bigger, the sky people would seal it up and winter would rule again. He kept gnawing away while dodging the sky peoples' arrows.

Autumn

Finally, an arrow struck Fisher on his tail. He rolled over and began to fall to Earth. Before he hit the ground, the great spirits lifted Fisher up. They placed him among the stars to mark his journey across the sky each year in honour of his bravery.

DID YOU KNOW?

The fisher is a North American forest creature related to the weasel. It eats small animals, but is actually not a fan of fish!

Guardians of the Great Flood

To South American Inca stargazers, the Milky Way was a river and the dark shapes within it were creatures who came to drink. One was Yacana, the llama – the Inca's most prized animal and the spirit that protected all llamas on Earth.

The myth of Yacana

According to legend, people had become cruel and greedy. They stole from one another, neglected their fields and never worshipped their gods. Only high up in the Andes Mountains did people still lead good lives.

Star signs

Two herders who lived in the mountains noticed that their llamas had stopped eating and were constantly gazing up at the stars. When the herders asked the animals what was wrong, they replied that the gods were angry with humans and would soon send a flood to destroy Earth.

The great flood

The herders quickly moved their families and flocks to the highest cave in the mountains. As soon as they were safe, the rain began to pour down. It was like nothing they had ever seen. Thunder shook the ground and lightning ripped across the sky. The people watched as the rivers flooded and the sea overflowed.

Safe and dry

As the waters rose, the mountains rose up too, keeping the families safe. Eventually the rain stopped. The Sun god, Inti, shone brightly and dried up the flood. The mountains sank back to their original places and the herders and their families returned to the land.

Guardian spirits

To this day, the llamas in the stars look down upon the world and remember the great flood. At night, they climb down from the sky and drink water from the ocean to stop the sea from ever overflowing again.

DID YOU KNOW?

Yacana's eyes are two of the brightest stars in the sky. Below it, a baby llama can be seen drinking from its mother.

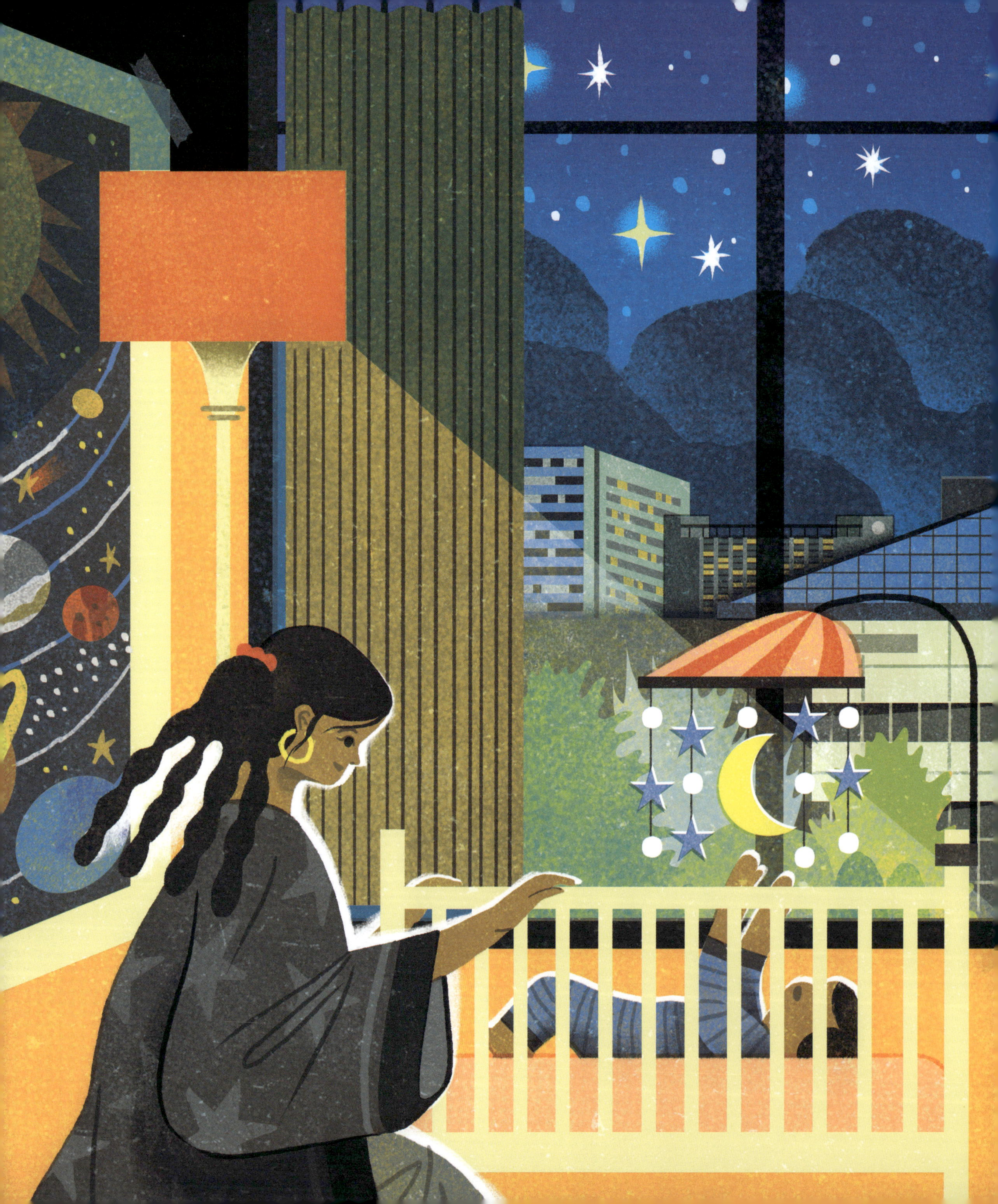

STARS AND US

Throughout our lives we are surrounded by stars. When we are young, stars in songs and stories comfort and soothe us. As we grow, stars in the sky guide us and inspire us. On Earth they are symbols of hope, stardom, identity and faith.

Celestial Navigation

Today, we can pinpoint exactly where we are on Earth with the help of satellites out in space. Early sailors only had the Sun and stars to guide them safely across the open ocean.

Navigation motivation

Navigation made it possible for people to explore new lands and trade goods with other countries. It helped fishermen to find their way home and enabled ships to reach foreign ports.

Rise and shine

The Sun and the stars move across the sky from east to west. Ancient sailors could work out where they were heading by tracking the stars throughout the night and during the different seasons.

Signposts in the sky

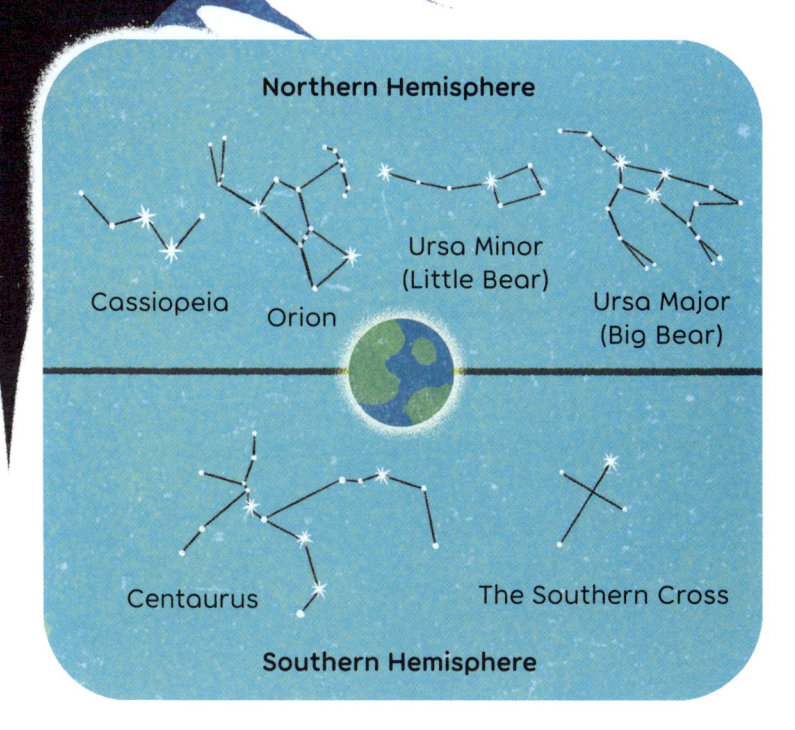

1. Follow the Sun

During the day, our star is a compass as it moves from east to west. It is possible to work out north, south, east and west using the shadows cast by the Sun.

2. Constant constellations

Constellations are groups of stars that create patterns in the sky. The Earth takes a year to move around the Sun and different constellations become visible throughout the year. Circumpolar constellations are ones that are always visible and useful for navigation.

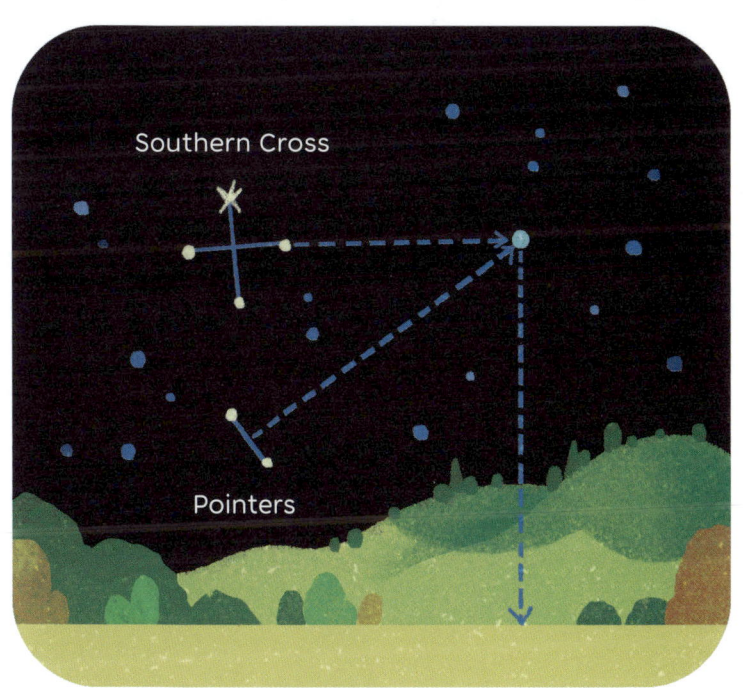

3. Finding north

The North Star, or Polaris, viewable in the Northern Hemisphere, sits almost directly above the North Pole and does not change position in the sky. Find it at the end of the constellation called the Big Dipper or the Plough.

4. Finding south

The Southern Hemisphere does not have a bright pole star to follow, but you can still find south using the Southern Cross. No matter the time of year, the four stars of the cross point due south when they reach their highest point in the night sky.

Inspired by Stars

The night sky has always been a source of inspiration to authors, artists, poets and composers. Some of the world's most famous works have stars at their centre.

Written in the stars

Space was shrouded in mystery in the 16th century. Stars and celestial objects are mentioned 400 times in playwright William Shakespeare's works. They are described as beautiful, constant and having the power to control human destiny. In *Romeo and Juliet* the characters are described as 'star-crossed lovers' because their fate suggests they can't be together.

Space traveller

The famous 1943 novel, *The Little Prince* by Antoine de Saint-Exupéry, follows a prince who learns lessons about life on his travels from planet to planet. Saint-Exupéry was an expert in navigating by the stars. The book's cover illustration, which he painted, shows the star Aldebaran with Saturn and Jupiter just as it would have appeared in the early 1940s.

Bright night

In 1889, Vincent Van Gogh completed the now world-famous painting *Starry Night* while he was recovering from mental illness. The scene was inspired by the view from his hospital room. The human world is shown in darkness and our eyes are drawn upwards to the swirling night sky with its glowing stars.

DID YOU KNOW?

Ella Fitzgerald's 'Stairway to the Stars', Elton John's 'Rocket Man', and 'Walking on Sunshine' by Katrina and the Waves have been played on the International Space Station to wake up the astronauts!

Symbols of Faith

Stars are among the oldest things we will ever see. Their constant and unfading light means that stars have come to represent hope, wisdom and a power beyond our world.

The Star of Bethlehem

In the Christian faith, the Bible tells of a bright star shining in the east that guided three wise men to the birthplace of Jesus.

For centuries, astronomers have searched for evidence of a bright star at that time. There are theories about a supernova, a comet, a solar flare and an alignment of planets that could possibly explain the Star of Bethlehem.

The Star of David

This ancient symbol has been used in many religions throughout history. It became connected with the Jewish faith in the 17th century and now appears on synagogues, tombs and the Israeli flag.

The star was used by the Nazis to mark out Jewish people during the **Holocaust**. It has since become a symbol of suffering and resistance.

Star and crescent

The star and crescent were first developed in Greek Byzantium in 300 BCE. It became the emblem of the Ottoman Empire, which began in modern-day Turkey in the 14th century.

Today the star and crescent appear on the Turkish flag as well as other national flags where the majority of the population follow Islam. The five-pointed star reflects the Five Pillars of Islam – faith, giving, prayer, pilgrimage and fasting.

Star Signs

Astrology is the belief that the positions of the Sun, Moon, planets and stars affect the character and lives of people. Even if you don't believe in it, you are more connected to the stars than you might think!

Aries (The Ram)
21 March–19 April

Pisces (The Fish)
19 February–20 March

Aquarius (The Water-Bearer)
20 January–18 February

Capricorn (The Sea-Goat)
22 December–19 January

Sagittarius (The Archer)
November 22–December 21

Scorpio (The Scorpion)
24 October–21 November

Ancient origins

The western zodiac signs are a result of the beliefs and observations of the Babylonians and Ancient Greeks more than 4,000 years ago. They did not know it then, but it turns out that stars are at the heart of what we are.

Made from stardust

Almost all the chemical elements that make up the human body were formed in stars! Planet Earth and everything in it, including the calcium in our bones and the oxygen in our blood, formed in the fiery deaths of stars.

Taurus (The Bull)
20 April–20 May

Gemini (The Twins)
21 May–21 June

Cancer (The Crab)
22 June–22 July

Leo (The Lion)
23 July–22 August

Virgo (The Maiden)
23 August–22 September

Libra (The Scale)
23 September–23 October

Western zodiac

Astrology followed in the western world has 12 signs. Each sign corresponds to one of the star constellations that exist in the zodiac – a belt of sky around the Earth.

Over a year, the Sun appears to move into different constellations. The dates in a **horoscope** are when the Sun appears in front of a particular astrological constellation. It is believed that a person's character is influenced by the sign of the date and time of their birth.

Show Time

Stars are brilliant, mystical and beyond reach. They are at the very top of our world, so it is no wonder that people who are famous for their achievements on Earth are called 'stars'.

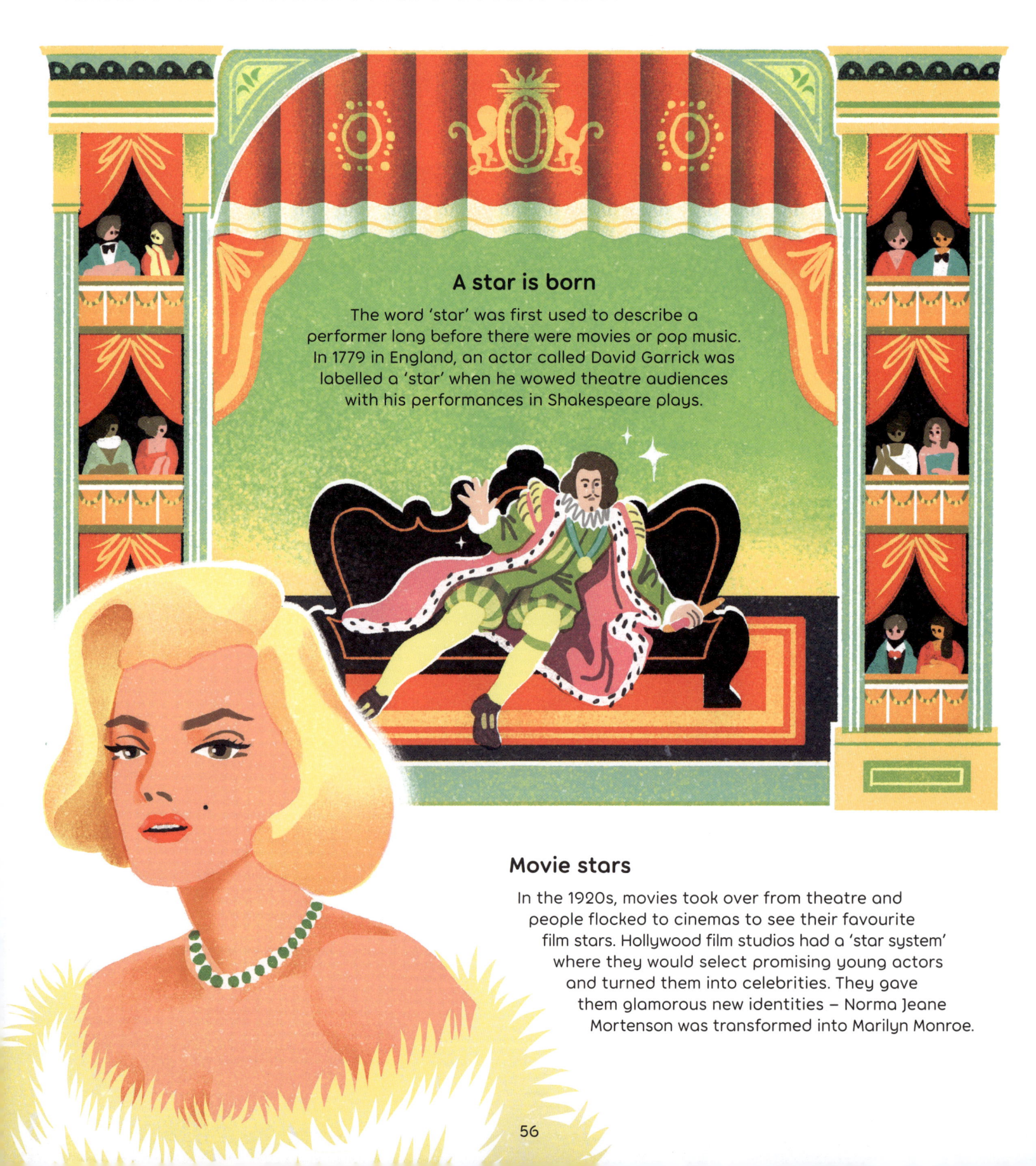

A star is born

The word 'star' was first used to describe a performer long before there were movies or pop music. In 1779 in England, an actor called David Garrick was labelled a 'star' when he wowed theatre audiences with his performances in Shakespeare plays.

Movie stars

In the 1920s, movies took over from theatre and people flocked to cinemas to see their favourite film stars. Hollywood film studios had a 'star system' where they would select promising young actors and turned them into celebrities. They gave them glamorous new identities – Norma Jeane Mortenson was transformed into Marilyn Monroe.

Megastars

In the 1950s rock 'n' roll music created a new kind of star. Elvis Presley was one of the first singers who rocketed to stardom. With more and more people owning a television, music, films and sports were beamed straight into people's homes.

ELVIS PRESLEY

WALT DISNEY

DID YOU KNOW?

The Walk of Fame is a pavement in Los Angeles, USA, studded with more than 2,700 stars. Each has the name of a star from the world of TV, theatre, film or music.

Starry Superstitions

The sight of a star shooting across the sky is so beautiful that it holds deep meaning in many cultures of the world. It can represent a human soul, or even hold the key to our hopes and dreams.

Bad luck

In Greek mythology, shooting stars were believed to be the god Zeus throwing stones down from the heavens when he was angry.

Good luck

In North America, Europe and Asia, it is widely believed that if you wish upon a falling star your wish will come true. This has its origins in ancient civilisations, when it was believed that shooting stars appeared when the gods opened the heavens to peer down at Earth. If you made your wish before the star disappeared, the gods would hear and grant your wish.

Free spirits

In areas of France, Germany, Poland and the United States a shooting star represents the souls of the dead departing for heaven. In Chile it is wandering souls looking for the right path, whereas in the UK it is the souls of babies being born into the world.

Myth buster

The science behind a shooting star is much less romantic. It is not a star at all, but a small piece of space rock or dust, known as a **meteor**. It hits Earth's atmosphere at great speed and heats up and glows as it moves. Most meteors burn up in the atmosphere before they reach the ground.

Glossary

Astronomer/Astronomy – the students and study of the Sun, Moon, planets and stars

Big Bang – the huge explosion that created the universe

Black hole – an area in space that pulls objects in, with gravity so strong nothing can escape

Celestial/cosmic – all things related to space

Cluster – a group of stars or galaxies that are close together

Constellation – groups of stars that create patterns in the sky

Core – the centre of a planet or star

Dark matter – invisible things in space that we can tell exist because of their gravity

Galaxy – a huge group of stars, gas, dust and planets

Gas – air-like matter

Hemisphere – half of the planet, divided into north and south

Holocaust – the mass killing of millions, especially Jewish people, during World War II

Horoscope – predictions about people's lives based on zodiac signs

Mass – the amount of matter in an object

Meteor – a burning space rock that streaks across the sky

Index

A
al-Balkhi, Abu Ma'shar 28
Andes Mountains, South America 44–5
Andromeda 19, 28, 34–5
Antoine de Saint-Exupéry 51
Aquarius 54
Aries 54
art 50–1
astrology 54–5
astronauts 16, 51
astronomers 15, 27–30, 52
Athena 35

B
Babylon 24, 54
Banneker, Benjamin 28
Bell Burnell, Jocelyn 29
Bethlehem, Star of 52
Beyoncé 57
Big Bang 31
Big Dipper (the Plough) 49
black holes 14, 17
books 50

C
Canada 42–3
Cancer 55
Cannon, Annie Jump 28
Capricorn 54
Cassiopeia 49
celebrities 56–7
China 21, 27, 38–9
clusters, star 19, 40–1
colours, star 13
constellations 24–5, 34–5, 39, 40–1, 43, 45, 49, 54–5

D
dark matter 19
David Garrick 56
David, Star of 53
dwarf stars 13–4

E
eclipses 27–8
Egypt 24, 26
Einstein, Albert 29

F
Fitzgerald, Ella 51
flags 53
France 59

G
galaxies 18–21, 25, 28–31
Galilei, Galileo 29
Gemini 55
Germany 59
gods, goddesses 27, 34–6, 38, 40, 44–5, 58
gravity 11, 17–19, 28

H
Hemispheres, North and South 25, 49
Hoffleit, Dorrit 29
Hollywood 56–7
horoscopes 55
Hubble, Edwin 29–30
hybrid stars 15

I
Incas 44–5
International Space Station 51, 57
Iraq 24
Islam, Five Pillars of 53

J
John, Elton 51

K
Kalahari Desert, Botswana, Namibia and South Africa 21
Katrina and the Waves 51
Khoi, Southern Africa 37

L
Leavitt, Henrietta Swan 28
Leo 55
Libra 55
life cycles 10–11, 14–15
light years 20
Little Prince, the 50
Local Group 19

M
main sequence stars 12, 14
Māoris, New Zealand 40–1
Marilyn Monroe 56–7
Massive stars 13–17
Matariki stars 40–1
Messier, Charles 28
meteor 59
Mexico 26
Milky Way 19–21, 25, 28, 36, 39, 44
moons 20, 26, 39, 54
music 51, 56–7

Navigation – finding your way from one place to another

Nebula – a space cloud where stars form

Nuclear fusion – where atoms smash together to create energy, making stars shine

Observatory – a building with telescopes and scientific equipment for watching space

Orbit – the path something takes around another

Pulsar – a fast-spinning, flashing star

Sacrifice – giving up something that you value so that something good may happen

Satellite – man-made space objects that sends us information

Solar – related to the Sun, like a solar eclipse

Solar system – our Sun and the planets that revolve around it

Supernova – a massive star's huge explosion

Superstition – a belief in luck or magic

Telescope – a tool to see far into space

Uv – standing for 'ultra violet' – invisible sunlight that can burn skin

Zodiac – star groups linked to birth signs

N
navigation 48–9
nebulas 11, 14, 20
neutron stars 14–17
Newton, Sir Isaac 28–9
North Star 42, 49
nuclear fusion 11

O
observatories 27, 29–30
Orion 24, 49

P
Perseus 34
photography, space 29
planets 20, 26, 28–9, 50, 52, 54
Polaris 42, 49
Poseidon 34
Presley, Elvis 57
protostars 11
pulsars 17, 29

Q
Qixi Festival, China 39

R
Reber, Grote 29
red giants 14
Relativity, Theory of 29
religion 52–3

Romans 34–5
Romeo and Juliet 50

S
Sagittarius 54
sailing 48
satellites 30, 48
Scorpio 54
seasons 25, 41, 48
Shakespeare, William 50, 56
Solar System 20
Southern Cross 49
spaghettification 19
star signs 54–5
Starry Night 51
sun god 27, 45
Sun, the 11, 14, 16, 20, 24–8, 30, 37, 45, 48–9, 54– 5
supergiants 13, 15
supernovas 14–16, 52

T
Taurus 55
telescopes 12, 29–31
timekeeping 26
Turkey 53

U
Ursa Minor/Major 49
USA 42–3, 56–7, 59

V
Vincent Van Gogh 51
Virgo 35, 55

W
Walk of Fame, Hollywood 57
Webb, James 30–1
Wolf-Rayet stars 15

Z
zodiac 24, 54–5

Ursa Major

Orion

Delphinus

Crux

Pegasus

Vulpecula

Tucana

Camelopardalis